A Help Hand

Written and illustrated by Shoo Rayner

Collins

Twiggy looked exactly like a stick. No one was able to see him.

Twiggy wanted a change. He wanted to be helpful.

So, Twiggy tumbled out of the bush where he lived.

An ant was trying to cross a ditch.

"May I help?" asked Twiggy in a jolly way.

"Can you make a bridge?" the ant asked.

6

Twiggy made a bridge.

The ant trudged over Twiggy's back and called, "Whee!"

The ant was in charge of a school outing!
One hundred and ninety six ant children galumphed
over Twiggy's back.

That's five hundred and eighty eight pairs of legs, and no please or thank you!

Twiggy's back ached. He walked on.

In a clearing, a slimy, slippery, ginger slug looked very hot and bothered.

"May I help?" asked Twiggy.

"Fetch a leaf for a sunshade," the grumpy slug whined.
"This scorching sunshine will dry me out."

Twiggy fetched a huge, heavy leaf. He held it over the slug as it wiggled its gooey, sticky way back home.

The slug slid under his cold, slimy, yucky house without a please or thank you!

Twiggy trudged on.
His back and arms ached.

Three angry beetles were trying to reach
a hairy berry.

"May I help?" asked Twiggy.

One beetle scrambled up Twiggy's painful back and stood on his aching head!

The beetle snatched the berry. "Catch!" he called to his friends.

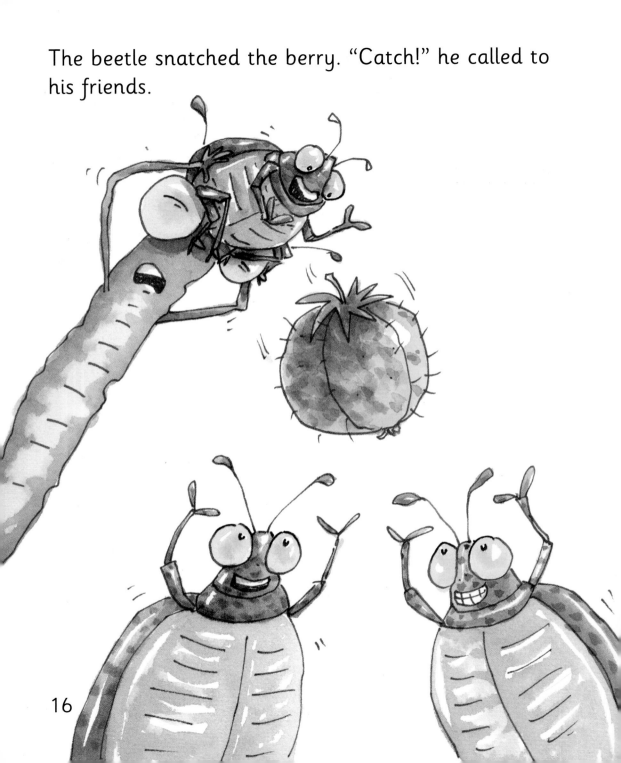

The beetles whizzed away with the berry without a please or thank you!

Twiggy's head ached.
Twiggy's arms ached.
Twiggy's back ached.

Twiggy struggled back to his bush.

Wedged in a branch, Twiggy looked exactly like
a stick.

"They'll have to fetch me if they want my help," Twiggy harrumphed.

However, Twiggy had discovered a new love for adventure.

"Where shall I go next?" Twiggy proclaimed, spying the greenhouse.

Helping

After reading

Letters and Sounds: Phase 5

Word count: 299

Focus phonemes: /ee/ y, e, ey /j/ g, ge, dge /oo/ u /w/ wh /v/ ve /igh/ y /c/ ch /f/ ph /ai/ a /s/ se /z/ se /l/ le /ch/ t, tch

Common exception words: of, to, the, one, were, friends

Curriculum links: Science: Animals, including humans

National Curriculum learning objectives: Reading/word reading: apply phonic knowledge and skills as the route to decode words, read other words of more than one syllable that contain taught GPCs; Reading/comprehension: understand both the books they can already read accurately and fluently and those they listen to by predicting what might happen on the basis of what has been read so far

Developing fluency

- Your child may enjoy hearing you read the book.
- You could each take the part of one or more characters. Encourage your child to think about the words used to describe how each character should speak and the appropriate expression (e.g. *Twiggy – jolly; Slug – grumpy, slow*)

Phonic practice

- Help your child to get quicker at reading multi-syllable words. Look at the following words:

  exactly   slippery   adventure

- Ask your child to:
  o Sound talk and blend each syllable "chunk".
  o Then read each chunk in turn.
  o Now read the whole word quickly.

Extending vocabulary

- Ask your child if they can think of a synonym for each of the following words:

  fetch (*get*)   wedged (*stuck*)   spying (*spotting*)   discovered (*found*)

  snatched (*grabbed*)   scorching (*sizzling*)   trudged (*tramped*)   tumbled (*fell*)